FYLATOS PUBLISHING

Publish on Demand, Inc.
© Fylatos Publishing,
Delaware 2017
Author: MELİH UĞRAŞ EROL
Editor: Konstantinos Fylatos
Photographs: Erdem Yalçın

© Fylatos Publishing
e-mail: contact@fylatos.com
web: www.fylatos.com

Pagination-Design: © Fylatos Publishing
ISBN: 978-618-5232-71-9

A Pinch From The Aegean

MELİH UĞRAŞ EROL

To my mother Şengül, and all other mothers...

FROM THE AEGEAN

They say "mothers are the best cooks in the world," and it was my mom who always saved the bottom of the pot from burning with her secrets during my cooking adventure. As a matter of fact, from whom can we learn when a ladle should meet a pot. Over time we all have considerably learned how a pinch can turn a meal into another flavor. It seems that the strongest spices are actually breath; onions are not tear, they are essences; a bite from a peppery meal is not pain, it is a pleasure; the thing that glares is not the taste of sour, it is joy; and that desserts can carry someone to another world over time.

Today, young people who travel around Agean can still see the stones which people spin to grind wheat; touch sieves made from bowel; witness the existence of ancient cabinets; taste a drop of olive oil obtained from a century old olive tree; and taste the fruit grown in the soil engaged with the agriculture in ancient times. That is the generosity and appreciation which Aegean presents to humanity. Aegean has always been a land on which different civilizations established; the food habits affected each other, and in fact, the food habits exist together. Naturally, it is not hard to express an opinion about the flavors of old times today, however, as a matter of fact, the main ingredients in Aegean such as olive, fig, grapes, pomegranate, vegetables, cereals and others still continue their existence.

In Aegean, cultures and cuisines are not stratified; they shall indeed identified together. Of course, it is impossible to mention the numerous methods and recipes in this few pages, however, in this book we inspired from couple of recipes and ingredients that you can hear if you visit neighborhoods of Aegean. In fact, Aegean has coasts, actually not opposite but coasts that live shoulder to shoulder. Aegean hosted lots of civilizations that had lived over its lands. The closest friend of Aegean region is undoubtedly Greece and Turkey. The closeness of their cuisines is like lifetime friendship. This friendship even can be witnessed in names of foods. For instance, eggplant called "patlıcan" in Turkish becomes "melitzána" in Greek; while in Turkish parsley is "maydanoz" Greeks call it "maïntanós" and so on. All these examples are just some pieces of evidence that shows how close are cuisines in Aegean. In fact, the similarity between the recipes is close and sometimes only the differences are on the used spices or kind of meat. Irreplaceable things underlie all of our shared values in Aegean.

The passion of cooking is hidden in one's heart. The matter is just getting into the kitchen and trying the ingredients, sometimes getting disappointed and sometimes throwing the plates to the air in joy. Of course being a local from Aegean region; living in this area, which has such a great, rich history; tasting its meals; feeling its textures made me feel closer to the passion of cooking. The chance of living in Aegean provided me to write this book by reinforcing my cooking adventure with passion. The starting point of this book is not, of course, undertaking today's terms, such as gourmet, or any other claim; it is just exploring and explaining the wealth of cooking together with the ability of cooking and being an Aegean local.

I inspired all of my recipes from the Aegean cuisine. Since I do not believe that any flavor occurs by itself, I do not also think that these recipes solely belong to me. You will see that these flavors benefit from the inheritance of the people living in Aegean land, who put various ingredients together to make delicious foods for centuries. Consequently, by feeling that these flavors and ingredients are in my genetic codes and the self-confidence of being from the Aegean region encouraged me to get into the kitchen.

I would like to thank my mother Şengül and to my father Cengiz, who have never spare their moral and material supports and trust. In particular, I would like to thank my brother Cemal Çağdaş, who enlighten the points which I could not see by his ideas; to Erdem Yalçın who always performed the final touch with his photographs, Gökçen Adar who encouraged me, our friends in Greece and Turkey. Lastly, I would like to express my gratitude to everyone who appreciates Aegean, the Aegean cuisine, and our friends from all over the world.

THE KINGS OLIVES and QUEENS FIGS OF AEGEAN

Olive and olive oil are the basics of the Aegean. The Agean region host various types of olives. Some of them are the best for producing olive oil while the others for tables. Most of the olive products in Aegean are unique. Aegean is full of association and peace. The commonalities of Aegean shows it self in olives. For example, the olive called Kalamata. Kalamata olive of the Greek coasts is called Eşek olive, which means donkey olive, in the Turkish coast. However people generally call it Kalamata because it comes from the Kalamata area, they also name it as Eşek olive because of its big size. It is famous with its endurance and big size. This olive is prepared for tables by the method of scratching. Do not underestimate because of its name; you know that the most beautiful eyes belong to donkeys, so this type is also as spectacular as them. Of course, it is impossible to give all the details from this much page. There are many types and methods of preparing olives and olive oil, which you can see when you visit olive groves in the Aegean region.

Production methods can also grouped in several ways. So, the most known olive storage methods are scratching, crushing, pickling and saddling. The olives, which are grouped and picked up by all the members of the Aegean family, are cultivated by various methods according to their types.

Scratching method can be applied on different kinds of olives. The damaged ones among the olives, which were picked up by hand and carried to the houses, must be picked carefully and let aside. Scratching method is made by scratching the sides of olives 2-3 times. They scratch the olives and then put the olives into water. After a while olives shall be taken into the salty water, which is prepared by adding 1-2 tablespoon rock salt into 1 liter water.

Crushed olives are one of the most delicious types. It is easy to make. This type can be applied by the help of a hammer or an oval stone. The olives are crushed by hitting their top parts . During this stage, you need to be gentle. You should not remove the seeds. You need to put the olives that are opened into a big jar and then fill it with water. You can freshen the water to avoid the moldy taste of the olives. The olives that became tasty are stored in the water.

The saddled method is for the black olives. The olives that become darker shall be put into big sacks and sprinkled salt. A massive stone shall be placed over the olives that are in the saddles. The olives release their sour fluid from the sacks that are turned upside down at regular intervals, and thus they absorb the salt well. For centuries, all of the Aegean region hosted different civilizations. It sounds impossible to believe that this is just a coincidence. It seems like the rendement, wealth of the soil; the variety of the flora made almost every civilization feel closer to this land. The Aegean lands are like blessed.

In this plentifulness figs also play a leading role. Figs represent fertility in ancient Greece. It is called as the fruit of heaven. Some motives in the ancient sculptures are originated from the fig. In fact, olives and figs are the kings and queens of this land. Figs have lots of various types in Aegean, like its area of usage. Figs are like olives. They can be used as ingredients in limitless products such as fresh fruit, dried fruit, delight, jam, cologne, cream, soap and many others. By the way, the gentleman called "male fig" should not be forgotten as one of the leading actor.

Fertilization is essential for figs. Co-star of this fertilization is "male fig" and its flies. Their duty is to fertilize the other figs with their flies. These male figs, which are picked up early in the morning, are strung to the pikes, and each of them is hanged on the fig trees. Flies come out from "male fig" on the evening time, and the flies get into other figs' bottom parts and the fertilization finishes. And over time the figs grow and become fruits that we eat.

The large yellow fruits smell excellent. The bumps that occur when you touch the fig trees remind you how difficult is growing as a fig. Figs sparkles in the gardens like it compete with the bright yellow sun. The color of this fruit, when you open it, is enough to be overwhelmed. This color is not certainly red or pink, it is such a color that you probably want to watch for a long time. It seems like hypnosis of colors. Figs taste like a dream that you want to feel all day. You can easily peel its skin. It has such a smell that you can lost yourself inside the fig seeds as long as you smell. Fig also has black colored types. The purplefall figs, has a purplish color. Its skin is multicolored. This purplish black type among all other green types reminds people the miracle of nature of Aegean once again. Of course, these beauties belongs to Aegean.

Aegean hosts various fruit and vegetables other than olives and figs. The number of the herbs and vegetables that picked up from the plains, hills and mountains is almost unlimited. The generosity of the Aegean Sea is a whole another issue. Aegean is a region that is full of various foods and plentifulness from its lands to its sea. It leaks oil and molasses from its mountains, honey from its meadows. Aegean means plentifulness.

Table of Contents

PILAFS, PASTAS and PIES

DESSERTS

BEVERAGES

SOUPS

LAMB'S QUARTERS SOUP

When you travel the hills of Aegean, you will see that there are lots of plants to eat. One of these plants is the lamb's quarter. After boiling lamb's quarters you can drizzle olive oil and lemon juice, however, people are also drinking its boiled water, which is sweet. So, we decided to make a bowl of soup from this plant from Aegean.

200 gr cleaned lamb's quarters
100 gram minced beef
1 onion
4 glass water
Salt
Olive oil

For seasoning
1 glass of yoghurt
1 tablespoon flour
1 egg yolk
1 tablespoon lemon juice

Put olive oil in a pan and start sautéing the minced beef and grated onion in a large pan. Clean the lamb's quarters by cutting the seedy parts and take only the fresh parts. Cut the lamb's quarters into 2-3 pieces and put into boiling water. After a while add the boiling lamb's quarters into the minced beef mixture with its water. Never change the water. Stir yoghurt, flour, egg yolk and lemon juice in another cup and mix very well. Take 3-4 tablespoon of the soup into the yoghurt mixture and continue to mix. When the yoghurt mixture starts to warm, pour it into the soup and keep stirring. Add a pinch of salt and cook for a short while until the soup thickens.

HOT AEGEAN SEA

1 white fish (sea bass or similar)	3 tomato	1/2 tea spoon peppercorn
150 gram calamari (cleaned)	1 clove of garlic	2 tablespoon Ouzo or Rakı
150 gram shrimp (cleaned)	1 lemon juice	Arugula
150 gram mussel meat (cleaned)	1/3 water glass flour	Salt
6 water glass water	1 dessert-spoon hot chilli pepper	Olive oil
2 onion	4-5 cardamom seed	

Put the fish, cardamom seeds and black peppercorns into 6 water glass of water. Boil all for about 9-10 minutes. Do not boil more. Take the fish from the water and clean. Put the fish meats a side. Put the head, bone, and tail back into the boiling water and cook for 30 minutes over low heat. Clean the shrimps, mussels and calamaris. Cut the calamaris into 2-3 pieces. Boil the calamaris, mussels and shrimps for a while. Grate the onions and tomatoes. Start cooking the onions in olive oil and after a while add the tomatoes. When tomatoes are cooked, add the meshed garlic and cook for a short while. Strain the boiling fish bone water. Put the flour into a pan, cook by stirring continuously until the flour changes colour. Add the cooked onion tomatoes, strained fish water into the flour and stir continuously. When it starts to boil, add the shrimps, mussels, and calamaris. Add the lemon juice, ground hot chilli pepper and rakı. Boil for 2 -3 minutes. Sprinkle minced arugula while serving.

GREEN LENTIL with DRIES BLACK-EYED BEAN

1 tea cup green lentils
2 tablespoons dried black-eyed beans
4 water glass water
1 onion
1 potato
1 carrot
Salt
Olive oil

For seasoning
1 water glass milk
1 egg yolk

For sauce
Butter
Ground red pepper

Boil the black-eye beans and set aside. Chop the onion and start sautéing in olive oil. Cut the potato and carrot, add to the pot and cook for a while. Add the lentils to the vegetables and mix. Add the water and cook until lentils can be crushed. Crush the cooked soup and strain, put back to the pot. Mix the egg yolk and milk. Add two tablespoons of soup to the mixture. When the mixture starts to warm up pour into the soup and mix well. Add the black-eyed beans and salt. Boil for a short while. Heat red pepper in butter and pour on the top of the soup while serving.

NOODLE FISH

Ladies in Aegean prepare noodles in summer. Ladies come together and ask from every family to save eggs from the pens. When the eggs are ready, they meet and buy flour. Early in the morning ladies come together, prepare noodles and share equally. These noodles are eaten all year long. We connected the Aegean sea with these noddles.

1 white fish (sea bass or similar)	1 teaspoon coriander seed	Olive oil
1 teacup home made fresh noodle	1/2 teaspoon ginger	
6 glass of water	1/2 teaspoon nutmeg	*For seasoning*
1 onion	2 bay leafs	1 egg yolk
1 carrot	Mint	1 lemon juice
1 celery root	Black pepper	
1 lemon juice	Salt	

Put olive oil in a pan and start cooking the diced onion, carrot and celery root. Mesh the coriander seeds. Add the coriander seeds, ginger, nutmeg and continue cooking for a while. Add the water, fish, lemon juice, and bay leafs into the mixture. Close the pan lid and boil at low heat. After 10 minutes take the fish and bay leafs from the soup. Clean the fish. Add the homemade fresh noodles and boil until they are cooked. Stir egg yolk and lemon juice until well mixed. Add 2 tablespoons of the boiling soup into the egg yolk and lemon juice sauce. Mix very well and when the mixture starts to warm up add the sauce into the soup. Put the fish meat into the pot and continue boiling. Continue to stir the soup add salt, black pepper and mint.

TARHANA or TRAHANA

We could not finish this chapter without sharing how to prepare this wonderful soup. Tarhana (or trahana) is prepared through different ways in the Aegean region; however, this recipe contains some common points that we all share. This recipe has a special herb. This plant, which can be collected from mountains, is special for the Aegean region called Tarhana herb.

4 kilo onion	1 kilo semolina	3 kilo strained yoghurt
4 kilo capia pepper	1 bunch of tarhana herb	Water
3 kilo tomato	(a unique plant available in Aegean)	Salt
2 kilo flour	2 water glass ground red pepper	

Tarhana is one of the flavors of Aegean cuisine. You can find many recipes in different locals. Almost every family in the region prepares this dry soup from summer. In some regions tarhana is in fist-sized chunks, in some areas mealy, in others in light color or dark orange.

Strain the flour and semolina. Mix and set aside. Chop the onions in a boiler. Add the chopped red peppers and chopped tomatoes. Place them all on fire. Cook for a while. After the ingredients start to cook, add 1-liter of water, tarhana herb and let it cook. Stir and mix the materials. When all the ingredients cook, take the tarhana herb from the mixture. Pour the semolina and flour into the mixture slowly. Meanwhile thoroughly mix all ingredients, flour, and semolina without stopping. Mix all ingredients to avoid agglomeration. Add salt, red pepper powder and mix well. Put the materials widely in a container and let to cool. After cooling add the strained yoghurt, mix well and let to rest for a night.

Next day, by a big spoon, divide the tarhana mixture into small parts, place in a large tray and let to dry under sun. When tarhana pieces start to dry, turn them upside-down for several times. Cut the tarhana pieces into small pieces to dry thoroughly. This process may take 2-3 days. When tarhana pieces are completely dry, strain, rub and crumble into small pieces with your hands. Do this for several times. Keep the tarhana in a cloth bag.

To prepare the soup cook the tomato paste in olive oil. Add water and add the prepared tarhana. Stir until boiling and boil for a short time until the soup thickens.

APPETIZERS & SALADS

HOMEMADE PICKLE

2 bands of rock samphire
Rock Salt
Vinegar
Garlic
Water

Pickles are delicious appetizers prepared during winter or summer time. Almost all kinds of vegetables even fruits can be pickled. While preparing pickles some vegetables can be boiled or left raw. For example, rock samphire, capers, and sea beans can be prepared by boiling for a very short period.

Clean the rock samphire by cutting the tough parts. Boil the rock samphire for a short time and put them into a glass jar. Add a clove of garlic. Pour the salt, water, and vinegar mixture and seal it. It is ready after approximately 15 days

NUTTY GRILLED EGGPLANTS

4 eggplants
1 red onion
20-30 gram peanut
1 clove garlic
1 teaspoon cumin
Olive oil
Parsley
Salt

Grill the eggplants, peel, and chop. Mix the eggplants with finely chopped red onion. Crush the peanuts in a mortar. Add the garlic and continue to crush. Add the olive oil in to the mortar and mix. Mix the eggplants with cumin, salt and peanut sauce in olive oil.

Sprinkle with chopped parsley.

VEGGIES with YOGHURT

10-12 green pepper
2 eggplants
2 zucchini
400 gram small fresh potato

1 tomato
1 cup buffalo milk yoghurt
 (or sheep's milk yoghurt)
2 cloves of garlic

Dry rosemary
Salt
Olive oil

Peel the eggplants and zucchinis in stripes. Cut them into circles. Sprinkle salt over eggplants to bring out their bitter water. After 20-25 minutes soak the eggplants. Cut the small fresh potatoes into two. Put them into a pan with a little olive oil. Close the lid and start cooking over low heat by stirring. When the potatoes are ready, add rosemary and salt. In another pan heat the olive oil. Fry the zucchinis, eggplants, and peppers. Chop the tomatoes into big pieces fry them in olive oil, add a pinch of salt and add crushed garlic. Take all of the cooked vegetables into a plate; serve with yoghurt and the tomato sauce. You can mix all of the vegetables with yoghurt and add tomato sauce on top.

GLITZY TRIPE

Tripe, one of the ingredients, that is used in Aegean cuisine. Mostly people in Aegean prefer to use calf tripe as an ingredient for soup. To recover your health a nice tripe soup is a must. Following the popularity of tripe we tried an appetizer that can go well with one of the wines from Aegean vineyards.

200-gram calf tripe
100 ml cream
1 white onion
1 clove of garlic
1 dessert-spoon sumac
1 dessert-spoon verjuice

1/2 bunch of parsley
Crouton
Capers pickle
Salt
Ground red pepper
Olive oil

Clean the tripe thoroughly or ask your butcher to do. Boil the tripe and chop into cubes. Cut the white onion and rub with salt. Pour its bitter water and mix with sumac. Put the chopped tripe and cream into a pan and start cooking. Stir well until the cream thickens. Just before taking it off the stove add verjuice, salt, and minced garlic. Put the croutons on a tray. First put the rubbed onions and later the cooked tripes over the croutons. Heat olive oil, add a pinch of ground red pepper and drizzle over the tripe. Sprinkle with the chopped parsley and pickled capers.

ARTICHOKE with FRESH PEAS

Artichokes are one of the starring characters of Aegean cuisine. Artichokes can be cooked in different forms. Artichoke with meat, stuffing artichoke leaves, mashed artichokes, and many others.

1 kilo fresh peas
5 artichoke bottoms
1/2 bunch of dills
1/2 lemon juice
Fresh walnut
Salt
Olive oil

Clean and trim fresh peas. Boil the fresh peas and artichoke bottoms. Put the boiled fresh peas into a bowl. Chop the artichokes bottoms and add into cooked fresh peas. Mince the dill and mix with the artichokes bottoms and fresh peas. Crush the fresh walnut, mix with olive oil and lemon juice. Season the salad with the olive oil mixture and salt.

SHEEP'S SORREL with SEA BEAN

From the beginning of spring until autumn the hills of Aegean hosts sheep's sorrel. It looks like ear of a sheep, so that's why we call it as sheep's sorrel. While walking over the hills of Aegean you can meet with some of them. Just try it. You will have a sour taste, less acidic than lemon, but aromatic. What a chance it is having this wild greenery, which we can eat fresh in the Aegean region.

2 bunch sheep's sorrel
200 gram sea bean pickle
10 sun dried tomato

1 clove garlic
Olive
Olive oil

Soak the dried tomatos. After a while you will see that the dried tomatos will soften and become less salty. Chop the sheep's sorrel and dried tomatoes. Crush the garlic. Mix all materials in a bowl and add sea bean pickle, olives, and olive oil. You can also add pickled capers. Instead of pickled sea beans, you can boil fresh ones.

PICKLE FROM THE BRIDE

Mother-in-law asked from the new bride to serve pickles during dinner. However the bride hadn't pickled any vegetables. To make her mother-in-law happy what she can do was prepare pickles as fast as she can. This was one of the stories we used to listen from our elders while having his recipe in summer nights.

2 eggplants
1 red pepper
4 green pepper
200 gram green beans
7 cloves of garlic

2.5 lemon juice
1/2 teacup vinegar
Salt
Olive oil

Peel the eggplants in stripes and chop. Sprinkle salt to bring out the bitterness of eggplants. After 20-25 minutes soak the eggplants by squeezing them with your hand. Clean the green beans and cut into medium sizes. After taking out the seeds of the peppers chop them. Put a pot of water to boil. First boil the peppers, beans, and then the eggplants. Strain the vegetables. In a separate bowl crush the garlic, add the lemon juice, vinegar, salt, olive oil and mix well. Pour the sauce over the vegetables.

CHEESY CUCUMBER ANISE

Anise is one of the most delicious and used spices in Aegean. People in the region use it for their recipes or beverages. Mixing anise with cheese and cucumber created a delicious recipe.

3 cucumbers
1.5 tablespoon cream cheese
150 gram hard cheese (as you wish)
150 gram farm cheese (unsalted)

2 clove of garlic
1.5 dessert-spoon dry anise
Olive oil

Grate a hard cheese with farm cheese. Crush the garlics. Add the cream cheese, garlics into the grated cheeses and mix. You can use a blender but be careful not to make the mixture juicy. Chop the cucumbers and add into the mixture. Season with dry anise and drizzle olive oil.

ONION LIVER

300 gram lamb liver
7-8 shallots
1 capia pepper
2 clove of garlic
3 tablespoon red wine vinegar
1 teaspoon ground hot chilli pepper

1 teaspoon cumin
Flour
Celery
Salt
Olive oil

Grill the shallots and capia pepper on the embers with their skin. Peel the shallots and capia pepper. Chop only the capia pepper. Clean the liver by trimming the veins and membrane like parts. Wash the liver until the blood totally gets out and chop. Dry and put livers into flour, and fry over high heat. In another pan place the olive oil, add a pinch of flour and stir well. Add the shallots and chopped capia pepper. After 1-2 minutes add the fried livers, minced garlic, cumin, ground hot chilli pepper, salt and fry only for another 1-2 minutes. Pour the red wine vinegar into the pan and fry for a last 1-2 minutes. Add the minced parsley while serving.

SHRIMP STEW

250 gram shrimp	2 clove garlic	Feta cheese
1 capia pepper	1 bay leaf	Olive oil
1 tomato	1 teaspoon lemon juice	

Combining fresh shrimps from Aegean Sea with Aegean cheese, fresh red capia pepper and tomato from your garden, and olive oil. While they are stewed in the oven you will smell and later taste this gastronomic beauty. Take the seeds of the red pepper and cut into a piece. Put the capia pepper into a single person stew and start to bake. Do not completely bake the peppers. Clean the raw shrimps. Except its head parts put the shells of shrimps, 1 clove garlic, bay leaf into a mortar and start mashing. Add olive oil slowly and continue to mash. Strain the olive oil mixture. Grate the tomato. Put some of the olive oil mixture into a pan and begin to cook the grated tomato. After a while add the other clove of crushed garlic and shrimps into the pan, cook for 2-3 minutes and add the lemon juice. Put the shrimps on the top of the lightly roasted pepper and put a thick slice of feta cheese on the top. Pour a little more from the olive oil mixture and cook until the cheese gets golden or brown.

GLASSWORT with BASIL

Not only inside of the Aegean Sea but also its coast-lines are full of plentifulness. One of the greeneries that grow up in the shores of Aegean Sea is glassworts. Glassworts are plants that can be found in coasts of Aegean Sea; that's why you can smell the sea while having them as a appetizer. They are vegetables that have tiny bones. So, you have to clean them before eating. You can imagine that fishes in the Aegean Sea are glasswort in the land.

2 bunch of glassworts
4-6 leafs fresh basil
4 branch of fresh onion
2 dessert-spoon lemon juice
Fresh yhyme
Currant
1 table spoon walnut
Olive oil

Boil and clean the glassworts. Mash the basil with a mortar. Put the olive oil, walnut and continue to mash. Do not put a lot of basil, otherwise, the sauce can be bitter. Add the lemon juice and a pinch of fresh thyme into the mixture. Chop the boiled glassworts and fresh onions. Mix the chopped glassworts and green onions with the sauce and add a pinch of currants.

POMEGRANATE CHICKPEAS

300 gram boiled chickpeas
1 pomegranate
5-6 dried tomato
3 slice pastrami
1/2 bunch dill
1 tablespoon

sour pomegranate syrup
1 tablespoon tahini
Cumin
Salt
Olive oil

Soak the chickpeas one night before cooking. Next morning boil the chickpeas. Steep the dried tomatoes for 40-45 minutes. Change the water occasionally. Deseed the pomegranate. Mince the dill, strained dried tomatoes, and pastrami. Mix the minced ingredients with chickpeas. In another cup mix the sour pomegranate syrup, tahini olive oil and pourover the chickpeas salad. Add a pinch of cumin and salt.

Mastic !

What a fascinating flavor, which can you use in your kitchens. Once upon a time Çeşme, Izmir was also producing it but today the famous Greek island called Chios is the main producer of mastic.

Mastic trees drop mastic and farmers are collecting them one by one. Mastic drops are like diamond pieces.

Cultivating mastic trees require care and love.

Chewing a mastic drop will refresh you. You will thank to nature for such a amazing taste.

MASTIC CHEESE ON PLUM

150 gram cottage cheese
150 gram hard cheese (low salty)
200 gram mild cream cheese
2 mastic pieces
10-12 purple plum

1/2 lime juice
10 leaf fresh mint
1/2 tea glass olive oil

Put the mastic pieces into the freezer. Mash and mix the cottage cheese, Izmir tulum cheese, and mild cream cheese. Crush the mastic pieces and mix with the cheese mixture. Rest the mixture in the fridge for 1-2 hours. Put the fresh mint leafs into the boiling water for 10 seconds and put them into the olive oil. Add the lime juice and mash all ingredients with a mortar until it becomes a sauce. Cut the pitted purple plums into circles. Put the cheese mix over the purple plums and drizzle the olive oil sauce.

BITTER ALMOND CELERY ROOTS

150 gram goat milk yoghurt with mastic
1 dessert-spoon mayonnaise
1 celery root and leafs
1.5 dessert spoons raw almonds
Bitter almond oil
Salt gram goat milk yoghurt with mastic
1 dessert-spoon mayonnaise
1 celery root and leafs
Bitter almond oil

You can find the mastic goat yoghurt in some of the markets. If you cannot find, crush a drop of mastic from Chios and mix with goat yoghurt. Chop the celery stalk. Grate the celery roots and put into the yoghurt. Mix the mayonnaise, celery stalk and other ingredients. Crush the raw almonds, add into the celery salad and mix well. Add a pinch of salt and bitter almond oil. You can set the amount of the bitter almond oil up to your taste.

FRESH COWPEA with SOUR APPLE

1/2 kilo fresh cowpea
3 sour apples
1 clove garlic
1 teaspoon vinegar
Salt
Olive oil

Clean the cowpeas and boil the fresh parts in deep water. Strain the cowpeas and put them into a bowl to cool. Dice the sour apples and mix them with the cowpeas. Mix the crushed garlic, vinegar, and olive oil. Add a pinch of salt and drizzle the olive oil over the cowpeas and sour apples.

CLASSY VILLAGE SALAD

1/2 kilo cottage cheese
2 cucumbers
3 green peppers
1 palm almond
10-12 leaf sweet basils

1/2 tee glass rock samphire
pickle
Salt
Olive oil

Dice the cucumbers, chop the green peppers and sweet leaf basils, mince the rock samphire pickle. Add all of them into the cottage cheese and mix. Mash the almonds with a mortar add to the mixture. Add the almonds to the salad and drizzle the olive oil. Add a pinck of salt and put the rest of the almonds over the salad.

MARINATE ANCHOVY (GAVROS MARINATOS)

Anchovy is not only famous in Black Sea region. People living in Aegean region and especially in the Greek islands prefer anchovy marine as a fish appetizer with ouzo. This is a recipe that we tried in Plomari, Lesvos.

1/2 kilo anchovy
Sea salt
Water
2 black peppercorns
Vinegar

Arugula
1 clove garlic
Olive
Olive oil

Clean the anchovies by taking out the guts and heads. Wash them and put into a glass bowl. Sprinkle plenty of salt over all sides of anchovies and pour water until the anchovies are covered. Salt will cook the anchovies so be sure that the amount of salt in enough. Add black peppercorns, close the top of the bowl and let in the fridge for 3-4 days. Be sure that the anchovies are ready to eat. Prepare the anchovies filets and put into another bowl. Add vinegar, minced arugula, garlic, olive and olive oil.

BEEFY CREAMY

350 gram green bean
250 gram bone-in beef meat
3 slice of bread
1 cup yoghurt
1 dessert spoon clotted cream
2 clove garlic
1/2 tea spoon black peppercorn
1/2 tea spoon grounded red pepper
1 dessert spoon crushed walnut
Salt
Olive oil

Put the beef into a deep pan and add water until it   passes
the meat. Add the black peppercorn. Close the lid and
boil. Clean the green beans, cut into 3-4 pieces and boil.
Strain the boiled green beans, mix with clotted cream and
stir. Be careful not to crush the beans. Pour some from the
broth to the bread crumbs. Mix beans, crumbs and salt.
Crush the garlic and mix with yoghurt. Cut the meat into
small pieces. Heat the olive oil in a pan add the red pepper and meat into the pan. Cook for a short while. Pour
the yoghurt on the beans and the meat on the yoghurt.
Sprinkle walnuts on top.

39

SUNBATHING FISHES

I tasted this appetizer in Chios Island. Lots of people were ordering black fishes on plates. I wondered what was this and rushed into the kitchen. They told me that this is one of their favorite appetizers. It is easy to prepare but need some time. I wish you could try it one day.

3-4 Mediterranean horse mackerel
Sea salt
Black pepper
Thyme
Olive oil

Clean the fish, take the head, bones and cut into two but let the fishes joined from their backs. Open the inner parts of the fishes and add fresh grounded sea salt, fresh grounded black pepper and thyme. Cover the fish with these spices. Let the fish to sundry fro 3-4 hours. The spiced parts shall see the sun. After 3-4 hours, by drizzling olive oil, grill the fishes.

TOMATO PASTE

The smell of tomatoes in the summer of Aegean region can be felt all around. Some of the tomatoes are for canning, some for drying, and some for tomato paste. None of the parts are wasted. The juice of these tomatos are served with ice that cools everyone. The master of the main dishes is the tomato paste, especially the homemade one.

10 kilo tomatoes
150- 200 gram rock salt
Olive oil

Chop the tomatoes in a bucket, put half the salt, cover the top with a cheesecloth and place it in the sun. Stir frequently with a large spoon until the tomatoes starts to become a puree. Mash the tomatoes and strain it with a colander. Put the puree into a cloth bag and let it filter the water. Put the strained puree into a wide tray and let it dry. Constantly stir after it dries put the remaining salt up to your taste. Share the tomato paste into glass jars, pour olive oil on their top and close the jar lid.

HURRY UP HOT TOMATO

1 kilo tomato
10-12 hot chilli pepper pickle
4 tablespoon fig vinegar
2 cloves of garlic
1-2 bay leafs
Thyme
Salt
Olive oil

Grate the tomatoes and strain, but keep some of its juice in. Chop the garlics. Mix the tomatoes, garlic, hot chilli pepper pickles, vinegar, a pinch of dry thyme and salt. Add the bay leafs and olive oil. Put the sauce into a jar and keep in the fridge. You can serve this sauce with grilled foods or breakfast.

MAIN DISHES

OKRA and FRESH COWPEA with PEAR

In summer villages of Aegean full with fresh vegetables and fruits. All summer we look forward to see okras and fresh cowpeas in our gardens. When the first crops are collected we cook them with meat or in stew. Using okra and fresh cowpea in such a fresh recipe seem to be a good idea. So, we tried them with a little sweet, pear, and sour, lemon. I would strongly recommend you to try this recipe at a summer night while smelling the Aegean Sea.

1/2 kilo okra	1 tomato	Salt
1/2 kilo of fresh cowpea	1 lemon	Olive oil
3 pear	1 sugar cube	
1 onion	2 bay leaf	

Chop the onions. Start sauteing the onions in olive oil. Add the chopped tomatoes and continue to saute for a while. Clean the cowpeas and okras. Cut fresh cowpeas into 2-3 parts. Add the cowpeas and okras to the pan. Cook for 3-4 minutes. Stir inwardly from the edge of the pan. Be careful not to crush the ingredients. Add the pears that you divided into 4-5 pieces and continued cooking. Place bay leaves on top of all the ingredients add salt, sugar, half teacup of water and half teacup of olive oil. Close the lid of the pan and cook for 20-25 minutes. Add lemon juice upto your taste.

PINEY GOAT

1 kilo goat meat
2 onion
3 tomato
50 gram pine nut
1 branch of fresh rosemary

2 bay leaf 1 lemon
1 sugar cube
2 bay leaf
5-6- black peppercorn
1 tablespoon red pepper

Salt

Olive oil

Put olive oil into the stew pan. Chop the onions and add into the stew pan. Add the goat meat over the onions. Repeat this until the onions and meats end. Place the chopped tomatoes on the top. Add the pine nuts, black peppercorns, ground red pepper, rosemary and a pinch of salt. Pour 1/2 teacup water and cover the top of the stew pan. Prepare a dough to cover the lid of the stew. Cover around the stew pan lid with the dough. Cook for at least 2-2.5 hours in 180 degree oven. You can cook over amber by burying the stew pan until it's half.

PHEASANT in POT

1 pheasant	5 allspice grain	*For marinate*	2 bay leaf
1 onion	5 black peppercorn	2 onions	Salt
1 carrot	1 tablespoon tomato paste	4 tablespoons olive oil	Olive oil
2 potato	2 water glass water	2 tablespoons vinegar	
4 wild sage leave	1 glass red wine	1 sugar cube	

Some animals are under protection, so you have to use livestock. Pheasant is one of these animals, you have to use breeding farms. Grate the onions, add olive oil and vinegar. Make a few scratches on the pheasants (not deep) and rub the sauce thoroughly. Let the marinated pheasants in refrigerate at least 12 hours. Heat the pan. Fry both sides of the pheasant for a short time. Chop the onion, carrot, potatoes and put in another pot. Add the pheasant into this pot together with its oil. Add the sage, allspice grain, and black peppercorns. When the pheasant starts to cook, add the water mixed with the tomato paste. When it begins to boil, add red wine. Close the lid and cook for at least 2 hours in low heat.

CORNELIAN CHERRIES in ROUND ZUCCHINI

Zucchini is another headliner in the Aegean cuisine. Frying grated zucchini, cooking zucchini as a main dish with minced beef, or stewing zucchini and many others. Zucchini is a product that you can use in many different recipes. Stuffed zucchini is one of the classics of Aegean cuisine. What we done in this recipe is adding cornelian cherries as sour.

4 round zucchini	1 teaspoon ground
1 water glass rice	allspice
100 gram cornelian	1 teaspoon dried mint
cherry	1 teaspoon ground
1 onion	black pepper
1.5 water glass water	Salt
1/2 teaspoon ground	Sugar
cinnamon	Olive oil

Remove the seeds of cornelian cherries and cut into small pieces. If you are using dry cornelian cherries, you shall let them soak and soften. Grate the onion. Mix the rice with the cornelian cherries, onion, 2 tablespoon olive oil, allspice, cinnamon, mint, black pepper, a pinch of sugar, and one teaspoon of salt. Cut top of the round zucchinis and carve them. Grate the carved parts of round zucchinis into the mixture. Fill the round zucchinis with the mixture and close top parts back. Place the stuffed round zucchinis into a pot. Mix the 1.5 water glass water and two tablespoon of olive oil. Pour over the stuffed round zucchinis and cook over medium heat until the round zucchinis soften.

BEETROOT BALLS

Beetroot is a famous ingredient in the Aegean region. Historically beetroot accepted as coming from Asia Minor, todays Anatolia, and Europe. For thousands of years beetroot is in use at Agean region. Although beetroot used to be a component for medicine, today with its delicious taste, people in Aegean use beetroot in many different recipes. Beetroot with yoghurt, with vinegar olive oil, or beetroot pasta are some of the popular recipes. In this recipe we hide beetroot as a surprise in the middle of meatball bowls.

500 gram minced meat	Ground red pepper	Cumin
2 onion	Izmir tulum cheese	Breadcrumbs
1 beetroot	2 tablespoon of tomato paste	Parsley
1 bunch of purslane	2.5 water glass water	Salt
1 egg	Black pepper	Olive oil

Grate one of the onions. Mix the onion, minced meat, cumin, black pepper, egg, salt and breadcrumbs until you get a thick paste. Let the mixture in the fridge for an hour. Chop the other onion and grate the beetroot. Clean the parsley and purslane. Take their fresh parts and chop. Start cooking the onion and beetroot in olive oil. Add the purslane, parsley ground red pepper and cook for a short while. Let it cool. Take pieces from the minced meat and give small bowl forms. Grill each of these meatballs for a short while. Put the meatballs on a baking tray and fill with the vegetable mixture. Mix the tomato paste with water. Pour on the meatballs filled with the vegetable mixture. Place one piece of Izmir tulum cheese on each meatball and bake at 180 degrees until the cheeses are golden or brown.

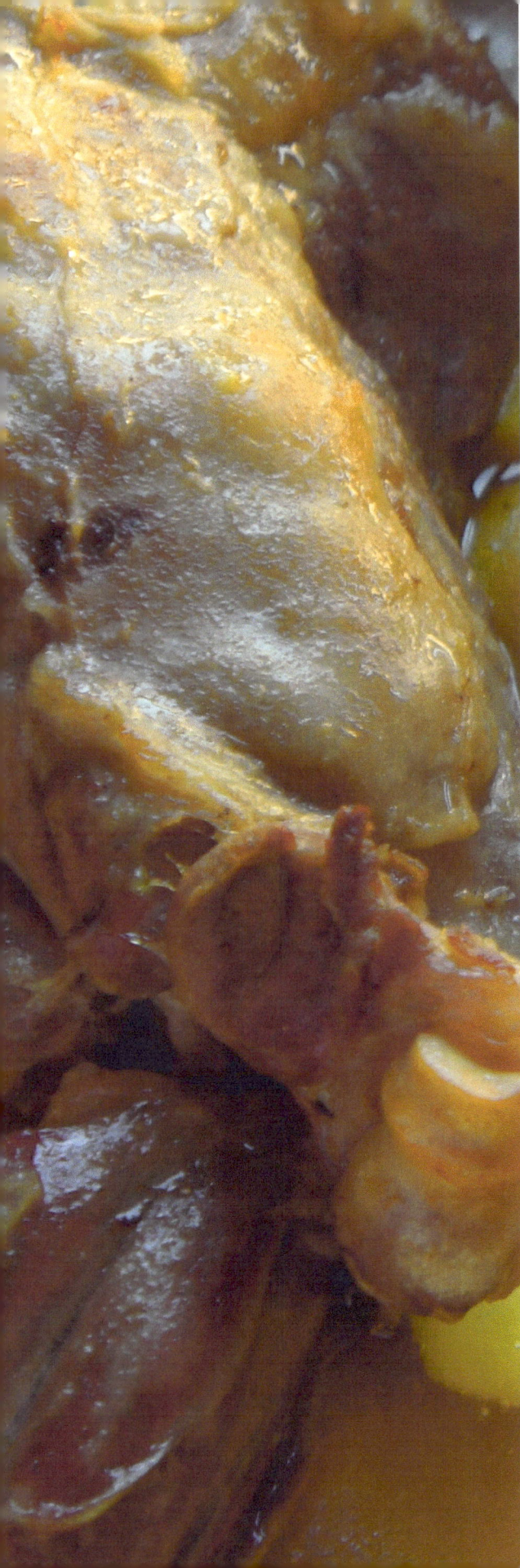

MUSTARD LAMB ARM

1 kilo lamb arm
1 onion
8-10 small fresh potato
1/2 bunch parsley
1 teaspoon black pepper-
corn
2 bay leaf

2 tablespoons mustard
powder
3 cloves garlic
Water
Salt
Olive oil

Chop the onion. Place the onion, parsley and lamb arm in a deep pot. Add bay leafs, black peppercorns, salt and five water glass of water into the pot and boil for about 45 minutes over medium heat. Cut the potatoes into two and place in a tray and drizzle olive oil. Put the lamb arm over the potatoes. Strain the broth and add into the tray. Cover top of the tray with baking paper and bake for 2 hours in 180 degree heated oven. Open top of the tray in the last 15 minutes, add the mustard powder and let the lamb arm roast.

SPLIT EGGPLANTS with FENNEL

Eggplants are mostly used in Aegean. Summer dishes with eggplants are unforgettable. This dish was one of the recipes you can see in most of local kitchens in Aegean. We added fennel to this recipe. Fennel is highly aromatic that is similar to anise. All through Aegean and Mediterranean you can find fennel in local open bazaars or in nature. Adding this flavorful herb into eggplant and mince made this classic recipe double up its taste.

5 eggplant	1 root fennel	5 green pepper
250 gram beef mince	2 cloves garlic	Water
1 onion	2 tomato	Olive oil

Peel off the eggplants stripped. With a knife make a thick line over the peeled eggplants, fry in olive oil and place in a tray. The line will get deeper after frying. Begin to saute beef mince and chopped onion in olive oil. Add chopped tomatoes. Add the finely chopped fennel, garlic, ground red pepper, ground black pepper, salt and continue cooking. Put the prepared mixture into the eggplants. Mix the tomato paste with water and pour over the eggplants. Cut the tomatoes into slices. Place the peppers and tomato slices over the eggplants. Cover top of the tray and bake in 180-degree oven. After a while, open top of the tray and cook until tomatoes and peppers are fried.

SUMMER BALLS

4 eggplant	1 egg	*For Sauce*
1 onion	150 grams of hard cheese	Yoghurt
1 potato	Breadcrumbs	Dried mint
1 zucchini	Salt	Fresh onion
2 cloves garlic	Olive oil	

Grill the eggplants and onion on the amber. Boil with the potato and zucchini. Mix and mash the eggplants, onion, potato and zucchini. Crush the garlics. Add the dice hard cheese, garlic, egg, breadcrumbs into the vegetables and make dough like mixture. Take small parts from the mixture; give ball shapes and fry in olive oil. Mix the yoghurt, finely chopped fresh onion and mint. Serve the fried balls with the yoghurt sauce.

ROLLED SEA BASS

6 fillets of sea bass

1 bunch of glasswort

150 grams of mozzarella cheese

1 clove garlic

1 dessert-spoon grated lemon zest

Black

Dried basil

Olive oil

Boil and clean the glassworts. It can be a little time consuming, so you better do it before start cooking. Prepare sea bass fillets (or ask from your fishmonger). Do not forget to take out the skin of the fishes. Carefully expand the sea bass fillets. Be careful not to damage the sea bass fillets. Cut the garlic and lightly rub into the sea bass fillets. Sprinkle the grated lemon zest, a pinch of black pepper and dried basil into the sea bass fillets. You may not use salt because the glassworts can be salty. Add the finely chopped glasswort and mozzarella cheese into the sea bass fillets. Wrap the filets by beginning from their large parts. You may stick a toothpick over the sea bass fillets to prevent leaking. Pour olive oil over the fillets bake in 180 - 200 degrees until the sea bass fillets are fired.

TURKEY RIBS on TARHANA HERB

The herb that we used in Tarhana from mountains of Aegean has a flavor that will make your kitchen commune with nature. The yellow and fresh parts of this herbal greenery hide a smell and taste that you will never forget. So, we thought why we are not using this classic flavor of Aegean in other recipes. Combining it with turkey was worth.

750 gram turkey rib
1 handful of tarhana herb
1/2 tea cup milk
1 onion
1 clove garlic
1/4 lemon

1 dessert-spoon curcuma
1 tea spoon honey
Salt
Ground black pepper
Olive oil

Grate the onion, crush the garlic in a large bowl and mix with milk, lemon juice, curcuma, olive oil, salt, honey and pepper. Thoroughly blend turkey ribs with the sauce. Let turkey ribs in refrigerator at least for 3 hours. Put tarhana herbs in a large baking tray. Cover tarhana herbs completely with turkey ribs. Pour the remaining sauce over turkey ribs. Close top of the baking tray with baking paper and bake for 45-50 minutes at 200 degree oven.

POTATO FISH

What would you do from fresh potato and fresh sardines from the coasts of Aegean? Of course mixing them together with herbs, corn flour, and frying in deep olive oil. You have to try frying it in olive oil. You will understand what kind of a festival will your palate feel.

300 gram sardines	2 tablespoon corn flour	Breadcrumbs
3 potato	1 dessert-spoon mint	Salt
3-4 branch of fresh onion	3-4 teaspoon ginger	Olive oil
1 egg	Ground black pepper	

Grate the potatoes. Mince the fresh onions and mix with the potatoes. Fillet the sardines and cut into small pieces. Mix the sardines and grate potatoes. Add the corn flour, egg, mint, ground ginger, salt, black pepper and mix well. Take small balls from the mixture; roll them in breadcrumbs and fry in olive oil. Add fresh onion on top while serving.

BULGUR in TOMATO

12 tomatoes
4 bunch green onion
150 grams of lamb mince
250-300 grams of spinach
1 teacup bulgur
Fresh mint
Parsley
Black pepper
Salt
Water
Olive oil

Cut top of the tomatoes. Carve the tomatoes and chop the carved parts. Mince the green onion, spinach, a pinch of mint and parsley. Mix all thoroughly the lamb mince and chopped tomatoes. Add olive oil, bulgur, a pinch of salt and back pepper into the ingredients and continue to mix. Fill the tomatoes with the mixture and close them back with their tops. Pour 1 teacup water and 2 tablespoon olive oil over the tomatoes. Bake in 180-degree oven for 40-45 minutes.

FRESH MOTTLED BEANS with DRIED PEPPER

Another tradition in Aegean is drying vegetables. When you visit Aegean villages in summer you can see that there are some vegetables hanged on balconies and walls of houses. You only need needle and thread. If you want to dry pepper you make a small scratch on peppers, thread the peppers and hang to sun until dried. With similar methods people in Aegean dry okras, eggplants, zucchinis, cucumbers, tomatoes and many others.

1/2 kilo mottled fresh bean	Grounded red pepper
1 onion	Sugar
2 tomato	Salt
8-10 dried red pepper	Olive oil
1/2 teacup water	

Clean and cut the mottled fresh beans. Chop the onion. Start cooking the onion and mottled fresh beans in olive oil. Stir and saute. Chop the tomatoes and add to the mottled fresh beans. Add the dried red peppers (without cutting), a pinch of sugar, grounded red pepper, salt and water. Close the lid and cook over medium heat.

OCTOPUS from GEORGINA

Friendly and generous people live in Molivos, Lesbos Island. Kısmet is a small family owned tavern offering exquisite cuisine of the Aegean in Molivos, Lesbos Island. In a summer day we cooked this delicious octopus with the owners of the tavern Georgina and Stratos.

5-6 octopus legs
1 onion
1,5 glass red wine
1 tablespoon allspice grain
3 bay leaf

2 desert spoon ground black pepper
Olive
Vinegar
Olive oil

Clean the octopus legs, take into a deep tinned copper pan and start cooking. Add the chopped onion, black peppers, allspice grains, and bay leafs. Stir occasionally and after it starts to cook add 1.5 glass red wine. Close the lid and wait until it boils. When it starts to boil add the olives and 3-4 tablespoon vinegar. Cook on low heat for 1-1.5 hours. Do not add water or salt. You can sprinkle parsley while serving.

GIANT ZUCCHINI

1 giant round zucchini
1 onion
1 cup fresh cowpea
2 tomatoes
Ground red pepper
Sugar
Salt
Olive oil

Put olive oil in a pan. Get slices from the giant round zucchini and chop. Add the chopped onion and diced cowpea on top of the chopped zucchini. Chop the tomatoes and put on the top of other ingredients. Cook over medium heat, stirring occasionally. Add ground red pepper, a pinch of sugar, salt and cook for a shorter period.

59

SOUR VINE LEAVES

In Aegean we also use vine leaves as an ingredient. When the first blossoms are seen, vineyards full with ladies collecting vine leaves. The fresh and green vine leaves are the best for stuffing. Vine leaves are generally stuffed with minced beef and rice. The sourish taste of vine leaves will freshen you like the gentle breeze of the Aegean. In this recipe, we also added plum and some others to make you feel the delicate of vine leaves.

Fresh vine leaves	Rosemary
350 grams beef mince	Black pepper
1 onion	Allspice
50 gram dried plums	Sugar
1/2 water glass verjuice	Salt
1/2 water glass water	Olive oil

Chop the onion and dried plums. Cook the onion and dried plums in olive oil for a short while and let it cool. Mix the beef mince with onion and plums. Add a pinch of salt, sugar, black pepper, allspice, and rosemary. Mix all ingredients. Take fresh leaves in boiling water and boil for 2 minutes until it changes colour. Take small pieces from the mixture and put into the leaves. Wrap the stuffed leaves like small bags. Place the stuffed vine leaves into a bowl, mix the water and verjuice. Pour the mixture over the stuffed leaves, close the lid and cook until stuffed leaves soften.

STUFFED COURGETTE FLOWERS

Another classic taste in Aegean is stuffed courgette flowers. At dawn, you have to collect the courgette flowers. Otherwise, after the sun rises the flowers close up and stuffing the courgette flowers will be harder. You can stuff courgette flowers with rice and many other spices.

15-20 courgette flowers	1 teaspoon mint	3-4 sour green plum
1 water glass rice	1/2 bunch dill	1-2 slices of lemon
2 onion	2 tablespoons currant	Salt
1 teaspoon ground cinnamon	2 tablespoons pine nut	Olive oil
1 teaspoon allspice	1 water glass water	

Clean the courgette flowers. Drain rice and soaking for 2 hours. Chop the onion and start cooking in olive oil. Add the rice and cook for 3-4 minutes. When cooking the rice stir constantly. Stir from outside to inside. Add salt, cinnamon, allspice, dried mint, pine nuts, and currants. Stir 2-3 times. Add 1 water glass of water and cook over low heat. Let to cool and add the minced dill. Add a small amount of olive oil in a pot. Take a teaspoon from the mixture and fill each of the courgette flowers. Put them into the pot. Divide the green plums into two and slice the lemon. Place the divided green plums behind the stuffed courgette flowers. Place 1-2 lemon slice at top. Fill half of the pot with hot water and cook over low heat for 20 minutes until the flowers soften.

IN THE FISH

2 medium white meat
fish
1 bunch of chard
1 onion
1 teaspoon orange zest
Halloumi cheese
Fresh mint
Fresh thyme
Muscat
Ginger
Salt
Olive oil

Chop the onion and chard. Start to saute them in olive oil. Add a pinch of finely chopped mint,thyme, orange zest, grated halloumi cheese and set aside to cool. Meanwhile, cut the fish until its dorsal fin, but do not fillet. Pour olive oil into the fishes, sprinkle a pinch of salt, ginger, and nutmeg. Put the vegetable mix into the fishes. Place the fishes on a baking tray and pour olive oil. Cook fishes in 180- 200 degree oven for 20-25 minutes.

LAMB COTTO with CAROB MOLASSES

500 grams medium fat beef mince
150 grams of lamb cotto
Carob molasses
1 egg
1 onion
1.5 dessert-spoon thyme

1.5 dessert-spoon black pepper
1.5 dessert-spoon cumin
2 dessert-spoon sesame
Breadcrumbs
Salt

Grate the onion. Mix the beef mince with breadcrumbs, egg, grated onion, thyme, black pepper, cumin, sesame, salt and knead. Rest the meat for an hour in the refrigerator. Put the minced meat mixture over a piece of baking paper or cling film. Extend the mixture as much as you can. Pour a little carob molasses, put a piece of lamb cotto and roll with the baking paper or cling film. Sprinkle a bit more sesame over the meatballs and grill.

FISH in SALT

1 kilo whole white fish	*For the sauce*
3 egg white	1 lemon
1 kg rock salt	1/2 water glass olive oil
1 kilo sea salt	Parsley
1/2 water glass water	Tarragon
1/2 water glass lemon juice	
2-3 branch fresh onion	
1 branch fresh garlic	
Pine oil	

Mix the egg whites, lemon juice, water, 4-5 drop pine oil, and salt. Mix all until you reach a paste. Put some of the mixture into the baking tray. Put the fish on the salt. Mince the fresh garlic. Place fresh onions inside the fish and add a pinch of fresh minced garlic. Completely cover the fish with the rest of the salt mixture. Bake at 200-degree oven for 30 minutes. For the sauce mince the parsley and a pinch of tarragon; mix with lemon juice and olive oil. Serve the fish with the sauce.

There are indispensable traditions in villages. One of these traditions are the wedding ceremonies of summer days in the Aegean province. Dining in weddings starts from 11 in the morning until afternoon 6. Almost 7-8 hours the host serve meal to visitors. One of the foods served during such ceremonies are the small rolls. Preparation of this dish begins 2 days before the ceremony. All of the women in the village gather at the wedding house. In big trays, the dough is kneaded and divided into hundreds of small rolls. These small rolls are prepared towards morning of the wedding day.

SMALL ROLLS with WALNUT

1/2 kilo minced beef	Olive oil	Water
1 egg		Yoghurt
2 water glass flour	*For sauce*	1 clove garlic
Black pepper	Tomato paste	Walnut
Salt	Ground red pepper	Olive oil

Mix and knead the minced meat, egg, flour, 1-teaspoon salt and 1-teaspoon pepper. You will get a little hard dough. Take pieces from the dough and give long shapes. Take some flour to your hands not to make the dough stick. With your hands, or with help of a knife, cut the long pieces into small pieces. They look like olives. Sprinkle plenty of flour into a tray and put the pieces in this tray. Stir occasionally by shaking the tray. Heat the olive oil in a pan. Fry the small rolls until their colour darkens. Set aside the fried rolls. In another saucepan start cooking the tomato paste with olive oil. Add ground red pepper and water until the sauce looks like a soup. Put the fried small rolls into the boiling water and cook until soften. Take the softened pieces into a serving dish and serve with the sauce. Mix the yoghurt with garlic. Pour the garlic yoghurt over the small rolls and sprinkle walnuts.

PILAFS, PASTAS and PIES

GRANDMUM ANTONIA OUZO BREAD

Grandmum Antonia and her family migrated to Lesvos Island after the population exchange between Greece and Turkey. Today her girl, grandchild and son of grandchild are living in Lesvos Island. They invited us for a lunch with all of their hospitality. We talked about their memories, had fun and eaten delicious foods cooked by them. This bread was one of the specials. Grandmum Antonia even used to win the first place in bread competitions organized in their church. Thank you Grandmum Antonia, mother Anna, grandchild Eri, and all.

2.5 water glass flour	*For scented yeast*
1 water glass warm water	2.5 water glass flour
1 tablespoon ouzo	1.5 water glass warm water
2-3 teaspoons sesame	8 gram yeast
1 teaspoon salt	1 teaspoon mahleb
1 tablespoon olive oil	

Take a porringer and start pouring the water inside. Add the flour, yeast and the mahleb. Stir by hand and when the mixture is kind of sticky stop stirring. On top pour by hand a little bit of water and a little bit of flour. Cover it with warm cotton fabrics, blankets or place it at a warm place for approximately 30 minutes. When it has risen it is ready for use. Take metal medium oven-ware and put inside a little flour and ouzo. Take the yeast that have already prepared and put it inside. Start to add the flour and while kneading by hand, add the water and salt. The mixture shouldn't be sticky in the fingers. If needed, more flour should be added. When the mixture is soft and looks united flatten it all around the pan and sprinkle on top of it, a little bit of water and some sesame. Bake at 180-degree oven for approximately 60 minutes. After the bread is cooked spread olive oil on the top.

COUSCOUS with BROAD BEANS

250 gram shelled fresh
broad beans
1 water glass couscous
1 tomato

1 onion
2 water glass water
1 tablespoon flour
1/2 lemon juice

2 cloves garlic
1 teaspoon sugar
Salt

Whisk thoroughly 2 water glass water, lemon juice and flour in a bowl. Put the fresh shelled broad beans into the prepared mixture. Chop the onion and saute in olive oil. Add the beans, with its water mixture, into the onion. Add salt, sugar and let to cook. Chop the tomato. In another pot cook the tomato in olive oil. Put the couscous into the tomato and stir 3-4 times. Sprinkle salt and add enough water (one finger over the couscous). Close the lid and cook the couscous. Crush the garlics. Mix the shelled fresh broad beans, couscous, and garlics.

SOFT CHEESE and FIG ROLLS

250 gram unsalted soft cheese
(you can chose type of the cheese)
2 thin sheet dough
4-5 dried fig
5-6 fresh mint leaves
2 tablespoon tangerine liqueur
1 egg yolk
Salt
Olive oil

Chop the figs and mint. Mix them with unsalted soft cheese. Add a pinch of salt. Buying unsalted soft cheese is important because you will decide the amount of salt. Cut the thin sheet of doughs into triangles. Apply the tangerine liqueur inside the pieces of the thin sheet doughs. Put the cottage cheese mixture into the pieces of the thin sheet doughs. Mix the olive oil and egg yolk. Brush the rolls with olive oil and egg yolk mixture. Bake in 180-degree until golden or brown.

WILD ASPARAGUS PILAF

It is possible to find different kinds of plants in the hills of Aegean. Among these plants wild asparagus is one of the most preferred one. Wild asparagus is used in different dishes, such as egg with wild asparagus. You can use wild asparagus in your every day meals. Wild asparagus is one of the essentials of an Aegean family. You can still collect them in the hills of the Aegean region.

1 bunch of wild asparagus
2 leek
1 water glass rice
250 grams shrimp
1/2 tea cup currant

1.5 water glass water
Lemon juice
Salt
Olive oil

Clean the prawns raw. Cut off the stems and take the fresh parts of wild asparagus. Clean the leeks. Chop the wild asparagus and leeks start to cook in olive oil. When the wild asparagus and leeks start to cook, add the rice. After a while add a pinch of salt, currant, two or three drops of lemon juice, shrimps and 1.5 water glass of water. Cook over low heat.

RED BREAD with LEEK

1/2 kilo flour
1 water glass milk
1.5 tablespoon dry yeast
4-5 leek

3 red peppers
3 tablespoons grounded red pepper
125 grams of halloumi
Olive oil

Mince the leeks, peppers, and halloumi cheese. Sift the flour. Mix the yeast and flour. Add 1 water glass olive oil and milk. Knead the flour until you reach a dough. Add all ingredients except the cheese and continue to knead. Cover it and let aside for approximately 30 minutes. After 30 minutes add the cheese into the dough. Pour olive oil into a baking tray and put the dough into the tray. Bake at 180-degree oven. When the bread is ready spread olive oil on the top.

TARHANA PASTA

We given the recipe of the delicious soup Tarhana (or Trahana). Here is another recipe tired and found with my family in Aydın, Turkey. Our village locates near the ancient city Magnesia. We prepare all of our stuff for winter in our tiny Aegean village. On a hot summer day, we made Tarhana (or Trahana). We saw that some of the ingredients remained. So, we founded this flavorsome pasta.

2 tomato	4 tablespoon semolina	Water
2 red pepper	1 teaspoon sugar	Salt
2 onion	1 egg yolk	Olive oil
A handful of tarhana herb	Brined goat cheese	
7 tablespoon flour	2 clove garlic	

Chop the onions, peppers, and tomatoes. Put all into a pot and add the tarhana herb. When the ingredients start to cook, add a little water. When all ingredients are cooked mash them (you can use a food processor). Strain the mixture and let it cool. Shift the flour and semolina. Add the egg yolk, salt and start kneading by pouring the tomato mixture into the flour and semolina. Continue until you reach a hard dough. Take small pieces from the dough and shape as a pasta. You can use a small stick to make penne. Boil water in another pot, add a little olive oil and cook the pasta. Crash the garlic and grate the brined goat cheese. Season the pasta with a little olive oil, garlics, and brined goat cheese.

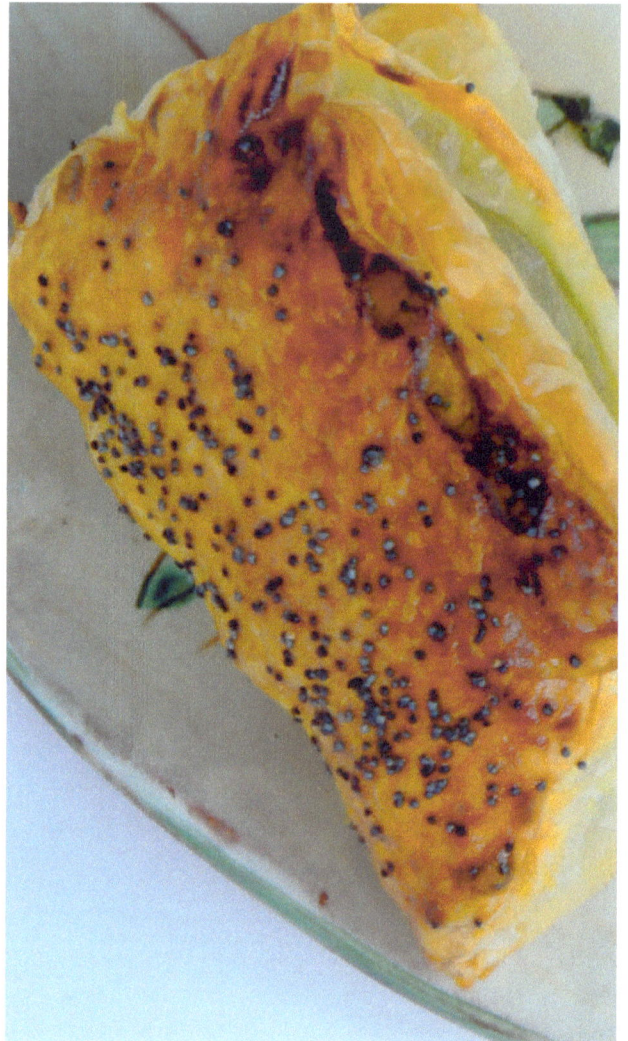

GREEN SHRIMP in PASTRY

6 puff pastry
250 grams of shrimp
1/2 bunch arugula
1/2 bunch chive

1 avocado
8-10 purple basil leaves
2-3 fresh garlic
1 egg yolk

Blue poppy seed
Olive oil

Clean the raw shrimps. Mince the arugula, fresh garlic, basil, and chive. Mash the avocado and mix with a little olive oil. Dip the shrimps into the avocado. Roll out the puff pastry, put some from the shrimps and minced vegetables. Wrap the puff pastry as you wish. Whisk the egg yolk and olive oil. Rub olive oil and egg yolk mixture over puff pastry, and sprinkle blue poppy seeds. Cook in 180-200 degree oven until golden or brown.

GRAPE JUICE CREPE

Sweet and salty, they are two main flavors of cuisines. You cannot isolate them from each other, just like the coasts and sea of Aegean. They are always side-by-side. Think where they are in your kitchens. The jars are shoulder-to-shoulder, just like the people Aegean. Why don't you try the sweetie rose jam with low salt soft cheese near the grape juice crepe?

2 egg
1 water glass flour
1 water glass milk
1 water glass grape juice

Salt
Rose jam
Low salted soft cheese

Whisk the eggs with a pinch of salt. Add milk and grape juice into the eggs and continue whisking. Slowly add flour into the mixture and beat until preventing agglomeration. Oil the pan. Pour a ladle of mixture into the pan and cook over low heat. Serve the crepes with the cheese and rose jam.

ARTICHOKE PILAF with FIG and MEAT

Here comes the queen of Aegean, the fig, and prince of Aegean, the artichoke in one pot. Adding meat to this recipe makes all of the tastes travel in our mouth. This recipe inspired from artichoke pilaf and pilaf with meat that we have during our festivals and celebrations. Thanks again to the Aegean cuisine to give us the opportunity to come out with such a recipe.

1 water glass rice	4-5 dried figs	Mint
250 grams of lamb meat cubes	1/2 water glass water	Cinnamon
3 artichoke bottoms	1/2 water glass milk	Salt
1 onion	1/2 bunch fresh dill	Olive oil

Soak the rice for 30 minutes. Strain the rice. Boil the artichoke bottoms al dente and chop. Chop the dried figs. Cook the lamb meat cubes with olive oil. Chop the onion, add to the lamb meats, and after a while add the rice. Stir once or twice. Sprinkle salt. Add the artichoke bottoms and dried figs. Mix the water and milk. Pour into the rice, close the lid and cook over low heat. Mince the fresh dill. Season the pilaf with mint, cinnamon, and fresh dill.

DESSERTS

A BITE OF LEMON GERANIUM

Flower in a dessert. Yes this is one of the flowers that you can see and eat in Aegean. This is a flower that you cannot imagine how it smells without tasting it. Gardens, pots, or balconies in Aegean can be full of this beauty. Making this dessert with this flower was unique.

4 water glass milk
1/2 water glass semolina
2 drops of mastic
10 piece of lemon geranium leave
Raw almonds

For syrup
1 water glass water
2 water glass sugar
2-3 drops of lemon juice

Cook the milk and semolina over low heat by stirring. When the mixture starts to boil put mastic drops and geranium leaves that you divided into 2-3 pieces. Stir consistency and cook until the mixture thickens. Get a bowl (2 finger deep), pour the mixture into the bowl and let it cool. When it reaches to room temperature let to cool in the refrigerator. In another pan mix the sugar, water, and boil until you reach a viscous syrup. If you wish, you can add 1-2 geranium leafs into the boiling syrup. Apply two or three drops of lemon juice and let the syrup cool. Cut a piece from the dessert, drizzle syrup and sprinkle crushed raw almonds.

MARJORAM APPLE

Marjoram, the symbol of happiness, is well known in Agean region. You can think a herb that is a mixture of pine, citrus, oregano and some more. Explaining it is a bit hard, but this is a plant that you can find all over the Aegean. The green and aromatic leaves is one of the best flavors for your drinks or desserts.

4 apples
1 tablespoon dried marjoram (or 4-5 sprig of fresh marjoram)
1 water glass water
1 glass sugar
1-2 drops of lemon juice

Boil the marjoram for 2 minutes in 1 water glass water, close the top of the pot and let the marjoram steep. Peel the apples, divide into two and take their seeds. Put the seeds into bottom of the pot. Put the apples into the same pot and sprinkle sugar over the apples. Strain the marjoram water and add into the pod. Close the pot lid, add 1-2 drops of lemon juice and cook over low heat until the apples soften.

STARCH PUDDING with
LIQUORICE ROOT JUICE

2 water glass milk
2 water glass water
1/2 water glass starch
1 teacup sugar
1 vanilla pod
1 teaspoon lemon zest
Nuts

For liquorice juice
1.5 liters of water
1 handful of liquorice root
(fibers)

Prepare the liquorice roots in fibber form (you can also buy in fibber form). Wash the liquorice roots for a short while. In a bowl add 1.5 liter of water and the liquorice roots, leave overnight. In the morning drain. Set aside two water glass of liquorice juice. Cut the vanilla bar into two and take the seeds. Put the milk and liquorice juice in a large saucepan and add starch. Start cooking over medium heat and stir constantly. Add sugar, vanilla seeds and lemon zest to the mixture and stir constantly. Pour the cooked pudding into a cup soaked with water and let to cool. Cut into pieces and serve with hazelnuts.

CHESTNUT LOUKOUMADES (or LOKMA)

The reality of life goes together with this recipe in the Aegean region. During marriage celebrations, funerals or death anniversaries people offer loukoumades (or lokma). Hosts offer visitors this traditional dessert. What we done is adding chestnut, which is commonly cultivated in Aegean.

1 water glass chestnut flour
1 water glass white flour
1.5 teaspoons of sugar
11 grams of dry yeast
4-5 chestnuts
1 water glass water
Salt
Frying oil

For syrup
2 water glass sugar
1.5 water glass water
4-5 drops of lemon juice

Boil the chestnuts, peel and crumble into small pieces. Mix the white flour and chestnut flour in a deep bowl. Mix the yeast with water. Mix the flours, yeast, sugar and a pinch of salt. Add water slowly and knead until you get a soft dough. Add the chestnut pieces into the mixture and continue to knead. Let it a side to leaven. In another pan mix the sugar, water and let it boil. Stir occasionally. Apply lemon juice and leave to cool. Heat the oil in a deep saucepan. Make small round pieces from the leavened dough and fry in hot oil. Stir gently while frying. When the pieces are fired dip into the syrup.

CAROB PIECES

Carob trees start from the southern Greece, Greek islands and till the middle of Turkey Aegean region are harvested. Instead of other powders, carob powder can be used in many different recipes. Carobs are hard and dark colored.

2 glass carob powder
2.5 glass flour
1/2 glass yoghurt
1 glass sugar
2 eggs
3 tablespoon walnut

1 dessert-spoon baking powder
1 dessert-spoon butterfat
1 water glass olive oil
Dried grape

Whisk the eggs, olive oil, and butterfat. Add the sugar and continue to whisk. Crush the walnuts. Add the yoghurt, flour, locust bean powder, baking powder, crushed walnuts and knead well until all ingredients mix. The mixture shouldn't be sticky in the fingers. When the dough is ready take pieces (walnut size) from the dough, roll and put over a baking paper. Place a dry grape over each piece. Bake at 180 degrees for 15 minutes.

ALMOND PUDDING with LAVENDER

Fragrant lavender, with it's purplish colour, which is harvested all around the Aegean land, can impress everyone. How about trying it in a dessert? Dried lavender gives an original taste inside the almond pudding, especially when it meets with orange zest.

3.5 water glass milk
1/2 glass sugar
1/2 glass almond
1/2 teaspoon orange zest
35 gram ground rice
2 dessert spoon dry lavender

Put the dry lavenders into a small linen bag or a covered strainer. Crush the almonds. You can crush them into big pieces. Put the milk, sugar, crushed almonds, ground rice, and the lavender bag into a pot. Stir the mixture and cook over medium heat. Stir constantly. When it starts to boil continue cooking until it thickens. Take the lavender bags from the pudding, add the orange zest and cook for 2-3 minutes more. Pour the pudding into small cups. Let them cool. You can add some more crushed almond on top.

PRICKLY PEAR SORBET

Think a fruit of cactus that does not require water but has a delicious taste. Prickly pear is what you are looking. This fruit has a beautiful orange color and is juicy. It loves sun and warm. Don't you think that it is an Aegean lover? What we tried from prickly pear is something that you would love to have on an Aegean beach.

4 (350 gram) prickly pear
1/2 water glass sugar
1/2 teaspoon ground cinnamon
2 teaspoons brandy

Pay close attention to thorns of the prickly pears. The thorns are thin and can be invisible. Show all your care not to hurt your hands. Use thick gloves, knife and fork. Open one side of the prickly pear, hold with fork and knife, roll and bring out the rind. Take the peeled prickly pears in a blender and mash. Strain and discard the seeds. Mix the mashed prickly pears with sugar. Stir until the sugar completely fed. Add cinnamon, brandy and mix well. Put the mixture into a large glass plate and place in the freezer. Stir the mixture every 30 minutes for 4-5 times. Let it all night in the freezer. Next day give roll shapes and serve.

BEVERAGES

MELON SEED JUICE

Using seeds to prepare a drink. This idea is a classic freshening that can be prepared quickly. Even in the Aegean region people are about to forget this delicious beverage. It is a perfect cold drink that you can have during long summer days of Aegean.

1 water glass of melon seeds
1/2 water glass sugar
4 water glass water
2-3 drops of rose water

Extract and gently scrape the fibrous parts of the melon seeds. Leave to dry. Begin to mash the melon seeds and mix it with sugar. You can use a food processor. Slowly add water into the melon seeds, continue to mash and stir. Strain the mixture through filter. You can add rose water before serving.

PEACH SHERBET
with SAFFRON

1.5 kilograms peach
500 grams sugar
5 water glass water
1/2 lemon juice
1 teaspoon honey
2 clove
1/2 teaspoon saffron

Peel and chop the peaches in a pan. Add the sugar, cloves, honey, lemon juice, water and boil for 30 minutes. Peaches shall be soften as much as possible. Add the saffron and let it cool. When sherbet comes to room temperature, strain and store it the fridge. Add ice into glasses while serving. yoghurt over the small rolls and sprinkle walnuts.

BLACK FIG LIQUEUR

1 kilo black fig
70 cl sugar-free vodka
1/2 water glass sugar
3 pieces dry clove
3 drops of mastic
1 cinnamon stick

Under normal conditions making liqueur takes at least 3 months but we speeded up the process. Let the mastic drops in the freezer for an hour and mash. Put half of the sugar in a jar. Divide black figs to 2-4 pieces and place over the sugar. Add the cloves, cinnamon, crushed mastics and the rest of the sugar. Pour the vodka into the jar. Close the lid and upside down the jar once a day. After at least 1.5-2 months strain the liquor into a bottle.

MELİH UĞRAŞ EROL

He was born in 1982, New York. His interest in food and cooking began during his childhood. While he was studying in Europe, his passion for different flavors advanced. Discovering tastes of countries was one of his enthusiasm. Throughout his cuisine and cooking passion, he never gives ups traveling and researching for food.

In his gastronomic interest and researches, he has fallen in love to the Aegean cuisine, once again. He continues to research, travel, even only for food, and cook.

He is producing his vegetables, fruits, beverages and olive oil in his small family field. He identifies himself as "only an Aegean." He believes that everyone can cook and invites everyone to the kitchen, his small family field and all over Aegean.

www.ingramcontent.com/pod-product-compliance
Lightning Source LLC
Chambersburg PA
CBHW042021080426
42735CB00003B/130